STEM

The Science of Fitness

Multiplying Fractions

Georgia Beth

Consultants

Lisa Ellick, M.A.
Math Specialist
Norfolk Public Schools

Pamela Estrada, M.S.Ed.
Teacher
Westminster School District

Publishing Credits

Rachelle Cracchiolo, M.S.Ed., *Publisher*
Conni Medina, M.A.Ed., *Managing Editor*
Dona Herweck Rice, *Series Developer*
Emily R. Smith, M.A.Ed., *Series Developer*
Diana Kenney, M.A.Ed., NBCT, *Content Director*
Stacy Monsman, M.A., *Editor*
Kristy Stark, M.A.Ed., *Editor*
Kevin Panter, *Graphic Designer*

Teacher Created Materials

5301 Oceanus Drive
Huntington Beach, CA 92649-1030
http://www.tcmpub.com

ISBN 978-1-4258-5815-5
© 2018 Teacher Created Materials, Inc.

Table of Contents

Stronger, Better, Faster

A swimmer reaches for the wall in record time. An artist stretches across a table as she draws. A family dances as they wash dishes. A firefighter hauls a hose up 10 flights of stairs. A dad lifts his son up to a jungle gym. We all depend on our bodies to perform at their best every day.

Around the world, scientists are peering into microscopes. They are reviewing data. Some of them observe world-class athletes as they sprint to the finish line. Others study **functional fitness**. They are devoted to making it easier for everyday people to lift heavy boxes, run to catch the bus, and play with their dogs. In the lab, on the track, or in the backyard, these scientists strive to understand the human body in new ways. The work they do pushes science forward. In the process, they make people stronger, better, faster. This is the science of fitness.

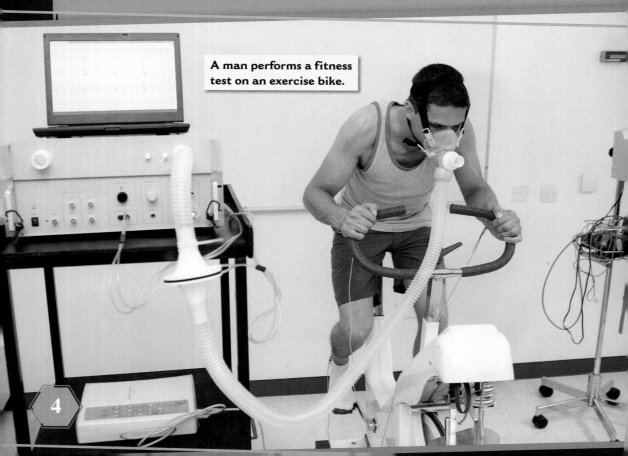

A man performs a fitness test on an exercise bike.

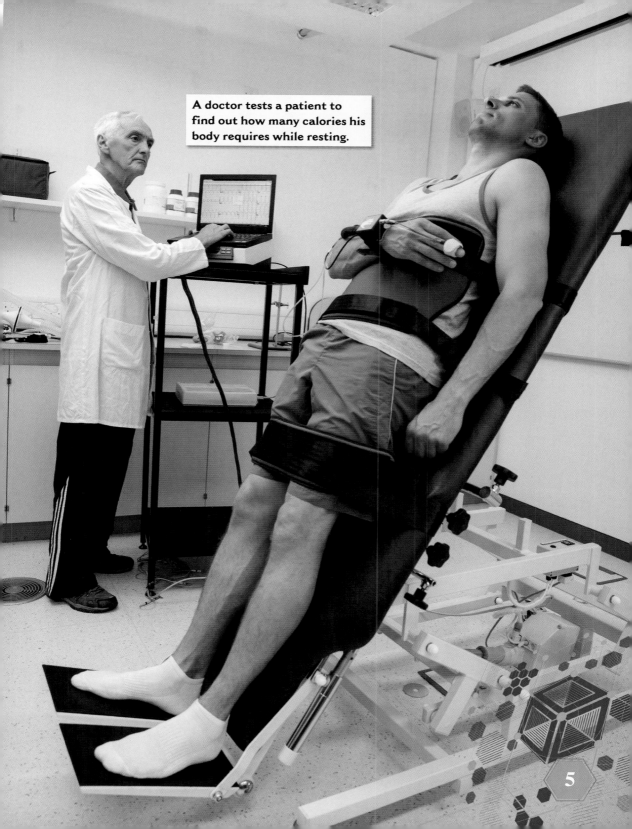

A doctor tests a patient to find out how many calories his body requires while resting.

Training and Performance

Some scientists study how athletes **exercise**. They observe people in labs where they can control the **variables**. Variables are things that might change. The temperature in a room might change. Athletes might change what they drink during workouts. Scientists need to control those things to get strong data.

Each study gives more information about what it takes to be fit. Scientists might track how much sweat athletes produce. They might focus on how long it takes to complete an exercise. The data makes sports safer. It helps people live longer. It helps people learn how to be healthier.

People must train to improve. Whether it's a student studying for a test or an athlete preparing for a big race, practice makes perfect. When it comes to fitness, performance improves when people train.

A man does push-ups during his crossfit workout.

Types of Training

Cardiovascular exercise, or cardio, gets hearts pumping hard and fast. It is an **aerobic** activity. Examples include dancing and biking. Parkour, Zumba, and zombie-inspired marathons keep hearts healthy, too. Cardio also helps people control their weight. It helps people prevent disease. Cyclists, runners, and triathletes all depend on cardio training to improve their bodies' ability to absorb oxygen. Training helps their muscles endure the demands of long races.

Parkour includes running, jumping, and climbing city obstacles.

LET'S EXPLORE MATH

Aerobic exercise increases lung capacity. One way to measure lung capacity is to take a deep breath and blow all the air into a balloon. Then, measure the width of the balloon through its center.

The width of Grace's balloon is 6 inches. Keenan fills his balloon $\frac{5}{8}$ as much as Grace does. Is the width of Keenan's balloon greater than or less than 6 inches? How do you know?

Anaerobic exercise is a way to build fitness. It burns fat and strengthens muscles. Strength training is a form of anaerobic exercise. It should be included as part of a complete fitness routine. Many people report that strength training makes them feel more confident. These workouts can even be done with a set of weights or resistance bands. But, your own body weight works well, too. Push-ups, squats, and planks build strength without other equipment. **Plyometric** workouts push muscles to work hard in short bursts. This form of strength training often includes jumping, hopping, and skipping.

Some workouts are aerobic and anaerobic. For example, **high-intensity interval training (HIIT)** is a popular training method. It mixes intense movement with short periods of rest. The goal is to increase heart rate in cycles. This mix strengthens the heart and lungs. It helps the body gain speed and power, and it gets better results!

Another type of exercise that is neither aerobic nor anaerobic is yoga. It still provides a workout. Yoga poses stretch muscles. The moves are usually done on mats. There is even a special yoga mat that works with an app to let people know if they are off balance.

Two people add dumbbells to their routine for higher intensity planks.

HIIT includes a mixture of activity and rest. During 6 minutes of Reggie's workout, he rests $\frac{1}{3}$ of the time. Use the model to write an equation showing how long he rests.

An athlete stretches her leg muscles to avoid injury.

Athletes want to improve their performance. But over time, bodies can **adapt** to training. What was once an intense workout can feel easy. Athletes shouldn't do the same workout each day. It is best to introduce new challenges.

New challenges might include trying a new sport. Train harder on some days, and do easier workouts on other days. Take a new class, or exercise with a friend. Push yourself to do something you've never done before. See how your body responds.

Experts also recommend that people stretch their muscles before exercising. Stretching helps blood move to muscles where it will be needed. Stretching helps athletes avoid injury so they can keep training. It also improves performance by increasing flexibility, which helps joints move more easily. Prior to stretching, people should jog or walk in place. These activities help muscles warm-up to make stretching safer.

Trainers remind their athletes that a workout does not end when the sweat stops pouring. Stretching offers many benefits. Stretching after a workout helps muscle stay long and lean. It can improve performance. It can also help increase blood flow to muscles.

A man jogs prior to stretching.

Rest and Recovery

Rest and recovery should be part of any training program. Rest is defined as the time when you are not training. Rest includes time spent sleeping. Sleep is an essential part of a training program. Want to be a stellar athlete? Sleep! Tennis champion Serena Williams goes to bed as early as 7:00 p.m. to help her body be at its best. Sleep supports mental and emotional health, too.

Recovery includes everything from stretching to reducing stress. Massages, heat wraps, and ice baths are tools that scientifically support the healing process. Drinking water and eating healthy foods help, too. Studies show that exercise causes small tears in muscles. After a workout, the body repairs the tears. This is how muscles get bigger. The process works best when there is time for muscle to rebuild before the next workout.

Some athletes train for speed. Others train for **endurance**. People's bodies need time to recover. Without proper rest, bodies get tired. Workouts may become too difficult. The result may cause a person to lose motivation. It may even lead to injury.

Football player Santana Moss takes an ice bath after training.

REM sleep is the stage of sleep when dreams occur. It is essential in helping people recover after a workout.

1. Adults spend about $\frac{1}{5}$ of their sleep in the REM stage. How much REM sleep does an adult get in 8 hours?

2. Adults spend about $\frac{9}{20}$ of their sleep in a stage called non-REM light sleep. Is this more or less than the fraction of time spent in REM sleep? How do you know?

3. How much light sleep does an adult get in 8 hours?

Nutrition

Food provides energy that athletes need to perform. Top athletes may need a shocking number of **calories**. Swimmer Michael Phelps once claimed to eat a whopping 12,000 calories a day when he was training for the Olympics. That's definitely outside of the norm.

Doctors recommend that meals consist of a healthy balance of foods. This balance includes filling our plates mostly with fruits and vegetables. These should take up about half of a plate at mealtime. About $\frac{1}{4}$ of the plate should have grains, such as brown rice and whole-grain bread. The last $\frac{1}{4}$ of our plate should include lean protein, such as fish or chicken. Healthy fats and dairy foods should be consumed in small amounts. Healthy fats include nuts and seeds, while dairy products include milk, cheese, and yogurt.

Many athletes eat a small meal or snack every few hours. When people eat, their bodies store **glycogen**. It's the fuel that gives people energy. About 2,000 calories can be stored at a time. But, some athletes need more fuel. That's why long-distance runners eat extra foods that give them added energy. They may even fuel up during a race with energy gels or sports drinks.

Dairy

Fruits   Grains

Vegetables   Protein

This hiker eats an apple for a healthy snack.

14

Michael Phelps

This food contains about 12,000 calories.

Macronutrients and Micronutrients

Every food is a mixture of water, **macronutrients**, and **micronutrients**. **Carbohydrates**, found in grains and fruit, are one type of macronutrient. They give bodies energy. Fats and proteins are also macronutrients. Nuts, avocados, and meat contain fat. Bodies use fat to support brain and bone health. Protein helps people feel full. Muscles use it to stay strong and repair tears. Meat, eggs, and seeds are all good forms of protein.

Micronutrients are important. But, they are only needed in small amounts. Micronutrients are vitamins and minerals that help bodies perform. Calcium builds strong bones. Vitamins A and C prevent infections. Iron helps keep bodies strong and provides energy. However, trainers may suggest **supplements** if an athlete's diet is missing a nutrient.

Supplements

Top athletes often take supplements to promote their health. Supplements help these athletes get the vitamins and minerals they need without having to eat all day. They might add protein powder to a smoothie or oatmeal. Or, they might take a multivitamin each day.

While body builders benefit from protein powder, most people get enough protein from food.

Many people read nutrition facts before buying food.

Vitamin D is another micronutrient. It helps bodies recover. Fish oil is a good source of vitamin D. It contains fatty acids that provide many benefits. It supports heart health. This vitamin also has been proven to help the heart and brain. And, it can even improve your mood.

Talk to a doctor before taking supplements. Supplements and vitamins that may seem harmless send about 23,000 people to the emergency room each year. Some experts also think there is a link between taking too many supplements and a higher risk of developing certain types of cancer.

Food Labels

The best way to stay healthy is to eat a wide variety of foods. It is important to avoid eating too many foods that have been processed in a factory. They are often loaded with extra sugar. They may have less fiber, too. Fiber is needed to help bodies digest food. Processed foods often lack micronutrients. They may also contain unhealthy types of fats. Food labels show the nutrients in packaged foods. These labels can help you make smart choices.

Nutrition Facts

Apple, raw

Serving Size 100g/3.5oz

Amount	% Daily Value
Calories 55	
Calories from Fat 1	
Total Fat 0.3 g	1%
Saturated Fat 0 g	0%
Trans Fat 0 g	
Cholesterol 0 mg	0%
Sodium 0 mg	0%
Carbohydrate 15 g	6%
Fiber 3 g	11%
Sugars 10 g	
Protein 0.2 g	
Vitamin A	1%
Vitamin C	8%
Calcium	1%
Iron	1%

The nutrition facts for an apple tell people how the fruit will fit into their daily meal plan.

Nutrition Facts

Marshmallows, candies

Serving Size 100g/3.5oz

Amount	% Daily Value
Calories 333	
Calories from Fat 2	0%
Total Fat 0 g	0%
Saturated Fat 0 g	
Trans Fat	0%
Cholesterol 0 mg	3%
Sodium 80 mg	27%
Carbohydrate 80 g	0%
Fiber 0 g	
Sugars 68 g	
Protein 3 g	0%
Vitamin A	0%
Vitamin C	0%
Calcium	
Iron	

How does the amount of sugar in the marshmallow candy compare to the amount in the apple?

19

Water

Did you know that the human body is mainly made up of water? Water is needed for all living things to survive. Water cools the body, helps blood circulate, cushions muscles and joints, and carries nutrients and oxygen to cells.

Hydration, or the process of absorbing water into the body, is essential for good health. Dehydration, or the process of losing water from the body, can be dangerous and unhealthy. Without enough water, the body cannot function properly. Breathing, sweating, and urinating all cause the body to lose water naturally.

Drinking water is a great way to stay hydrated. Water can also be found in solid foods. Fruits and vegetables, such as cucumbers and strawberries, contain a lot of water.

There are a variety of ways to check hydration levels. Clear or pale urine means that someone is fully hydrated. Dark urine often results when people need more water. A sweat **sensor** is a high-tech method to test whether someone is getting enough water. This sensor, or patch, sticks to the body and records how much sweat is produced. Then, it tells how much water is needed.

Adults need to drink about 8 cups (2 liters) of water per day. However, most athletes need to drink 10 to 15 c. (2.4 to 3.5 L) of water a day, depending on their training. Athletes need fluids, such as water, to have enough energy to compete. Fluids improve performance and recovery.

An athlete wears a sweat sensor that sends data to a smartphone.

Tran is a runner. She tracks how much water she drinks to be sure she is fully hydrated.

1. On a training day, Tran drinks 3 liters of water. How many $\frac{1}{2}$-liter bottles of water does she need to drink to meet her hydration goal? Write a multiplication equation to prove your solution.

2. Tran drinks $\frac{1}{4}$ of a $\frac{1}{2}$-liter bottle of water as soon as she wakes up. Use the area model to write an equation showing what fraction of a liter she drinks.

Training Tools for Athletes

There's no doubt that exercise, nutrition, and rest are essential to fitness. But did you know that mental training is also important? Scientists are now studying how athletes can give their minds a workout, too.

Fencer Miles Chamley-Watson trains with an app to improve his focus. He uses his brain to control the game. When his brain waves show that he is focused, a character moves across the screen. When he loses focus, the character stays still. The game helps him train his brain to pay attention. This is a good skill to have when a sword is aimed at you!

Athletes can also train their minds through **meditation**. They can focus their minds on an image of themselves having a good game or race. Meditation can help athletes become more aware of their strengths and weaknesses. People who meditate are often more relaxed during stressful situations. They also sleep better and recover faster.

Mindfully working out may help even casual fitness fans. Paying attention to each muscle may prevent injury. It can also keep people engaged as they train, helping them enjoy working out more.

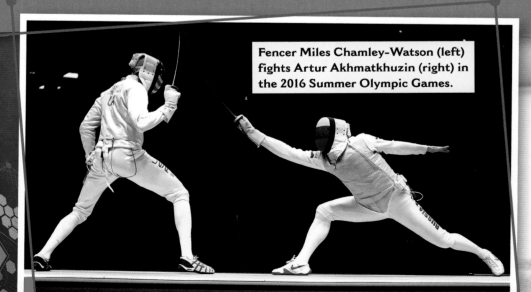

Fencer Miles Chamley-Watson (left) fights Artur Akhmatkhuzin (right) in the 2016 Summer Olympic Games.

Marlene's yoga class is $\frac{3}{4}$ hour long. She meditates for $\frac{1}{5}$ of it. What fraction of an hour does Marlene meditate? Draw an area model and write an equation to show your thinking.

This woman sits in the lotus pose, a cross-legged position used in yoga and meditation.

This woman uses her smartwatch to monitor her personal fitness.

It is said that knowledge is power. That might make personal fitness trackers the king of sports. These small **devices** help people record their activity levels. Fitness trackers have sensors that track movement. Some trackers measure heart rate. A few trackers encourage athletes to meditate. Trackers act as a visual cue to work out and eat healthy foods. At the end of the day, it's easy for a person to see how much they've moved.

Fitness trackers are easy to wear around your wrist or on your clothes, and they send data to a smartphone or website. Many gyms use trackers to encourage athletes to compete with one another.

Scientists are testing which tracking models work best. Designers are giving them the high-fashion touch, too. But, trackers may soon be invisible. Clear sticky patches could be the next wave of trackers. They will be able to measure everything from blood sugar levels to impact. This may help athletes avoid head injuries. Whatever shape they take, trackers give valuable information to keep people moving.

Fitness apps are useful for tracking progress.

Lily's goal is to walk $\frac{4}{5}$ of a kilometer without stopping. Every day her new fitness app tracks the fraction of the goal she meets before stopping to rest. How far does Lily walk each day?

Day	Fraction of Goal Met	Distance Walked (km)
1	$\frac{1}{3}$	
2	$\frac{2}{5}$	
3	$\frac{3}{4}$	
4	$\frac{9}{10}$	

An athlete jumps over a hurdle.

The Future of Fitness

Scientists are developing new ways to enhance fitness and health. One group of scientists created a scanner that can tell how many carbs you need to eat and when you should eat them. Columbia Sportswear Company's Omni Freeze Zero T-shirt cools the body during a workout.

Interested in a workout with no actual working out? One interesting new method is the Cyclic Variations in Adaptive Conditioning (CVAC) machine. It may look like a pod that an astronaut might sleep in, but it's not. The pressure inside the pod changes to compress and relax the body. Blood, organs, and muscles behave as though they are high in the mountains, where air pressure is low. Some people claim a few sessions a week can boost fitness as much as intense workouts.

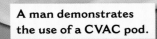

There will always be new ways to improve. The best thing to do is to properly care for our bodies. That means eating healthy food, getting exercise, and taking time to rest. The science is clear that these things are essential. The future of fitness is now!

A man demonstrates the use of a CVAC pod.

⚙️ Problem Solving

Selena and her friends walk one lap around the track behind their school. Selena wears a fitness tracker to record their activity, and it works perfectly! But, she forgets to wear it in the three situations below. Her friends are relying on her for the data. Help Selena use her data about one lap to calculate the following information each time she forgets to wear her tracker:

- distance
- number of steps
- time
- number of calories burned

1. One afternoon, Selena and her friends have some extra time. So, they walk three laps around the track.

2. They only walk half a lap before it starts to rain. They wait underneath a tree for Selena's mom to pick them up.

3. During a week's vacation, they walk two laps each day for five days.

One Lap Around the Track

Distance	$\frac{1}{4}$ mile
Number of Steps	500
Time	$\frac{1}{6}$ of an hour
Number of Calories Burned	25

Glossary

adapt—change to function better

aerobic—type of exercise that strengthens the heart and lungs and uses oxygen

anaerobic—type of exercise that builds muscle and does not use oxygen

calories—units of heat used to measure energy from food

carbohydrates—substances found in food that give bodies energy

cardiovascular—involving the heart and blood vessels

devices—equipment designed to serve a purpose

endurance—the ability to do something for a long time

exercise—to do physical activity for health and fitness

functional fitness—exercises or movements people do as part of their everyday lives

glycogen—a type of body fuel broken down into glucose, a type of sugar which is an energy source

high-intensity interval training (HIIT)—exercise that alternates intense periods of movement with brief periods of rest

macronutrients—carbohydrates, proteins, and fats the body needs to be healthy

meditation—the act of spending time thinking and reflecting quietly

micronutrients—vitamins and minerals the body needs to be healthy

plyometric—type of training that involves jumping, hopping, and skipping

sensor—a device that detects movement and transmits a signal

supplements—things added to something else to make it complete

variables—things that can change

Index

Answer Key

Let's Explore Math

page 7:

less than 6 inches; Explanations will vary but may include that if 6 is multiplied by a fraction less than 1, the product must be less than 6.

page 9:

$\frac{1}{3} \times 6 = \frac{6}{3}$, or 2 minutes of rest

page 13:

1. $\frac{8}{5}$ or $1\frac{3}{5}$ hours

2. More; $\frac{9}{20}$ is greater than $\frac{1}{5}$ because $\frac{1}{5} = \frac{4}{20}$.

3. $\frac{72}{20}$ or $3\frac{12}{20} = 3\frac{3}{5}$ hours

page 21:

1. 6; $6 \times \frac{1}{2} = 3$

2. $\frac{1}{4} \times \frac{1}{2} = \frac{1}{8}$ liter

page 23:

$\frac{1}{5} \times \frac{3}{4} = \frac{3}{20}$

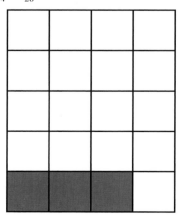

page 25:

$\frac{4}{15}$ km; $\frac{8}{25}$ km; $\frac{12}{20}$ or $\frac{3}{5}$ km; $\frac{36}{50}$ or $\frac{18}{25}$ km

Problem Solving

1. $\frac{3}{4}$ mi.; 1,500 steps; $\frac{3}{6}$ or $\frac{1}{2}$ of an hour; 75 calories

2. $\frac{1}{8}$ mi.; 250 steps; $\frac{1}{12}$ of an hour; $12\frac{1}{2}$ calories

3. $\frac{10}{4}$ or $2\frac{2}{4} = 2\frac{1}{2}$ mi.; 5,000 steps; $\frac{10}{6}$ or $1\frac{4}{6} = 1\frac{2}{3}$ hours; 250 calories